Poecabulary

Francis DiClemente

©2025 Francis DiClemente

Author's Note

Obsessed with vocabulary, I created this work as wordplay—an exercise to incite imagination and elicit connections in the reader's mind. I consider the word pairings a hybrid of vocabulary and poetry, which could be labeled as "Poecabulary" or "Voetry."

Contents

A 8
Abhor/Adore 9
Abjure/Adjure 10
Abortion/Adoption 11
Anima/Animus 12
Apoplectic/Apologetic 13
Autistic/Artistic 14

B 15
Barley/Barely 16
Bassoon/Buffoon 17
Bedlam/Beldam 18
Bibulous/Bilious 19
Breach/Breech 20
Bully/Buddy 21

C 22
Calm/Clam 23
Celery/Celerity 24
Comfort/Confront 25
Complaint/Compliant 26
Compulsion/Compassion 27
Conscious/Conscience 28

D 29
Dairy/Diary 30
Defective/Detective 31
Delitescent/Delicatessen 32
Diffident/Different 33
Disability/Durability 34
Disparate/Desperate 35

E 36
Emphasize/Empathize 37
Endanger/Engender 38
Endue/Ennui 39
Erection/Ejection 40
Expect/Except 41
Extricate/Extirpate 42

F 43
Factious/Factitious 44
Fertility/Futility 45
Forfeit/Forfend 46
Fornication/Fortification 47
Forsaken/Forgiven 48
Forward/Froward 49

G 50
Gambol/Gamble 51
Genealogy/Gynecology 52
Generals/Genitals 53

Generic/Gender 54
Genus/Genius 55
Gluten/Glutton 56

H 57
Halt/Hate 58
Haven/Heaven 59
Hew/Hue 60
Home/Hope 61
Human/Humane 62
Hurt/Heart 63

I 64
Imitate/Intimate 65
Immorality/Immortality 66
Imperious/Impervious 67
Ineffectual/Intellectual 68
Injure/Inure 69
Invisible/Invincible 70

J 71
Jackal/Jacket 72
Jealousy/Jeopardy 73
Jocular/Jugular 74
Joyful/Joyless 75
Jubilation/Justification 76
Juniper/Jupiter 77

K 78
Karma/Kismet 79
Kerflooey/Kerfuffle 80
Kindle/Kindness 81
Kiss/Kids 82
Knot/Know 83
Kook/Koan 84

L 85
Lair/Liar 86
Leave/Live 87
Leopard/Leotard 88
Lessen/Lesson 89
Licorice/Lickerish 90
Lonely/Lovely 91

M 92
Malady/Melody 93
Marry/Merry 94
Maturation/Masturbation 95
Meddle/Mettle 96
Meritocracy/Mediocrity 97
Morality/Mortality 98

N 99
Nap/Nape 100
National/Notional 101
Naval/Navel 102

Negate/Neonate. 103
Negligee/Negligent. 104
Nervous/Niveous. 105

O 106
Oblivious/Oblivion. 107
Obtuse/Obtrude. 108
Obverse/Observe. 109
Obviate/Ovulate. 110
Occlude/Occult 111
Orgasm/Organism. 112

P 113
Passable/Passible 114
Patience/Patients. 115
Peremptory/Promontory 116
Perfection/Perception. 117
Prevent/Pervert. 118
Purlieu/Puerile 119

Q 120
Quality/Quiddity 121
Quaver/Quiver 122
Quick/Quip. 123
Quiescence/Quintessence 124
Quiet/Quite. 125
Quixotic/Quizzical. 126

R 127
Rapine/Repine 128
Recalcitrate/Recalculate. 129
Redemption/Retention 130
Reject/Respect. 131
Rescue/Recuse. 132
Resent/Repent 133

S. 134
Salve/Slave 135
Scarcity/Sanctity 136
Selfish/Selfless 137
Silver/Sliver 138
Solid/Stolid. 139
Sympathy/Symphony 140

T. 141
Timber/Timbre 142
Tortuous/Torturous. 143
Tousle/Tussle 144
Tried/Tired. 145
Trivial/Travail 146
Turbid/Turgid. 147

U 148
Umbra/Umbrage 149
Unbearable/Unbeatable 150
Unconformable/Uncomfortable. 151

Understate/Understand 152
Untied/United 153
Upbeat/Upset 154

V. ... 155
Vacillate/Vaccinate 156
Venal/Venial 157
Veracious/Voracious 158
Vicious/Viscous 159
Victorious/Vainglorious 160
Violet/Violent 161

W ... 162
Waffle/Woeful 163
Wander/Wonder 164
Weather/Whether 165
Welder/Welter 166
Womb/Wound 167
Wraith/Wrath 168

X ... 169
Xenia/Xenon 170
Xenophobe/Xenophile 171
Xeric/Xebec 172
Xiphoid/Xyloid 173
Xylan/Xylene 174
Xylograph/Xylophone 175

Y ... 176
Yak/Yam 177
Yawl/Yowl 178
Ying/Yang 179
Yoke/Yolk 180
Yore/Your 181
Yucky/Yummy 182

Z. ... 183
Zap/Zip 184
Zeal/Zen 185
Zeitgeist/Zygote 186
Zenith/Zither 187
Zephyr/Zeppelin 188
Ziti/Zucchini 189

A

Abhor
Adore

Abjure
Adjure

Abortion
Adoption

Anima
Animus

Apoplectic
Apologetic

Autistic Artistic

B

Barley
Barely

Bassoon
Buffoon

Bedlam
Beldam

Bibulous
Bilious

Breach
Breech

Bully Buddy

C

Calm
Clam

Celery
Celerity

Comfort
Confront

Complaint
Compliant

Compulsion
Compassion

Conscious Conscience

D

Dairy
Diary

Defective
Detective

Delitescent Delicatessen

Diffident
Different

Disability
Durability

Disparate
Desperate

E

Emphasize
Empathize

Endanger
Engender

Endue
Ennui

Erection
Ejection

Expect
Except

Extricate
Extirpate

F

Factious
Factitious

Fertility
Futility

Forfeit
Forfend

Fornication
Fortification

Forsaken
Forgiven

Forward
Froward

Gambol
Gamble

Genealogy
Gynecology

Generals
Genitals

Generic Gender

Genus Genius

Gluten
Glutton

Halt
Hate

Haven
Heaven

Hew
Hue

Home
Hope

Human
Humane

Hurt
Heart

I

Imitate
Intimate

Immorality
Immortality

Imperious
Impervious

Ineffectual
Intellectual

Injure
Inure

Invisible
Invincible

Jackal
Jacket

Jealousy
Jeopardy

Jocular
Jugular

Joyful
Joyless

Jubilation
Justification

Juniper
Jupiter

Karma
Kismet

Kerflooey Kerfuffle

Kindle
Kindness

Kiss
Kids

Knot
Know

Kook
Koan

Lair
Liar

Leave
Live

Leopard
Leotard

Lessen
Lesson

Licorice Lickerish

Lonely
Lovely

M

Malady
Melody

Marry
Merry

Maturation
Masturbation

Meddle
Mettle

Meritocracy
Mediocrity

Morality
Mortality

N

Nap
Nape

National
Notional

Naval
Navel

Negate
Neonate

Negligee
Negligent

Nervous
Niveous

Oblivious Oblivion

Obtuse
Obtrude

Obverse
Observe

Obviate
Ovulate

Occlude
Occult

Orgasm
Organism

P

Passable
Passible

Patience
Patients

Peremptory Promontory

Perfection
Perception

Prevent
Pervert

Purlieu
Puerile

Quality
Quiddity

Quaver
Quiver

Quick Quip

Quiescence
Quintessence

Quiet
Quite

Quixotic
Quizzical

R

Rapine
Repine

Recalcitrate
Recalculate

Redemption
Retention

Reject
Respect

Rescue
Recuse

Resent
Repent

S

Salve
Slave

Scarcity
Sanctity

Selfish
Selfless

Silver
Sliver

Solid
Stolid

Sympathy Symphony

T

Timber
Timbre

Tortuous
Torturous

Tousle
Tussle

Tried
Tired

Trivial
Travail

Turbid
Turgid

Umbra
Umbrage

Unbearable
Unbeatable

Unconformable
Uncomfortable

Understate
Understand

Untied
United

Upbeat
Upset

V

Vacillate
Vaccinate

Venal
Venial

Veracious
Voracious

Vicious
Viscous

Victorious
Vainglorious

Violet
Violent

W

Waffle
Woeful

Wander
Wonder

Weather
Whether

Welder
Welter

Womb
Wound

Wraith
Wrath

Xenia
Xenon

Xenophobe
Xenophile

Xeric
Xebec

Xiphoid
Xyloid

Xylan
Xylene

Xylograph
Xylophone

Y

Yak
Yam

Yawl
Yowl

Ying
Yang

Yoke
Yolk

Yore
Your

Yucky Yummy

Z

Zap
Zip

Zeal
Zen

Zeitgeist
Zygote

Zenith
Zither

Zephyr
Zeppelin

Ziti
Zucchini

About the Author

Francis DiClemente is an Emmy Award-winning filmmaker who lives in Syracuse, New York. He is the author of multiple poetry collections, most recently *The Truth I Must Invent* (Poets Choice, 2023) and *Outward Arrangements: Poems* (independently published, 2021). His blog can be found at francisdiclemente.com.

www.ingramcontent.com/pod-product-compliance
Lightning Source LLC
Chambersburg PA
CBHW071202070526
44584CB00019B/2886